Alzheimer's

...There is hope

Alzheimer's
...There is hope

SHEILA ROBERTSON

CREATION HOUSE
A STRANG COMPANY

ALZHEIMER'S... THERE IS HOPE by Sheila Robertson
Published by Creation House
A Strang Company
600 Rinehart Road
Lake Mary, Florida 32746
www.strangbookgroup.com

Unless otherwise noted, all Scripture quotations are from the King James Version of the Bible.

Scripture quotations marked NAS are from the New American Standard Bible. Copyright © 1960, 1962, 1963, 1968, 1971, 1972, 1973, 1975, 1977 by the Lockman Foundation. Used by permission. (www.Lockman.org)

Design Director: Bill Johnson
Cover design by Amanda Potter

Library of Congress Control Number: 2009934258
International Standard Book Number: 978-1-59979-916-2

First Edition

09 10 11 12 13 — 9 8 7 6 5 4 3 2 1
Printed in the United States of America

CONTENTS

DEDICATION

It is my goal to live a dedicated life to my Lord and Savior, Jesus. Therefore, any accomplishments, success, or biblical insights that I have belong to Him.

I would also like to honor the three most important people in my life.

For Hubert, my husband—It has been a wonderful twenty-six-year adventure. I can truly say that there has never been a dull moment! You are my very best friend and the perfect husband for me. I love you.

For Mama—We've laughed and cried our way through life together. You're not only a great parent, you're also a great friend and I love you.

For Daddy—You were an incredibly steadfast influence on my life and I long to see you again. I love you and miss you so much.

INTRODUCTION

THE STUDY OF ALZHEIMER'S AND ITS MANY different indicators has been on my mind for several years. Recently, this dreaded disease hit close enough to home that I was motivated into action. The Bible references are mostly from the King James Version. The only reason for this is the fact that my concordance and Greek/Hebrew references are keyed to King James. When there was no need to analyze a word in its original language, I used the New American Standard. There are many good, new translations. These just happen to be the two that I used.

I pray that you would be encouraged by this book and that it would give you hope. Remember, all hope is in Jesus.

—SHEILA

Chapter 1

WHAT IS ALZHEIMER'S?

*A Look at the People at Risk and the Three
Major Symptoms of the Disease*

ALZHEIMER'S IS THE MOST SINISTER DISEASE OF our day. The pathology of this disease is uncertain. Scientists in the medical profession know what happens inside the brain to produce Alzheimer's, but they don't know what causes the change to occur. When medical science can't find a logical explanation as to why millions of people in the last fifty years have developed a condition in the brain known as Alzheimer's, then it's time to look somewhere else.

In 1901, Dr. Alois Alzheimer, a German physician, was treating a woman that was admitted to the hospital by family members. This woman was only fifty-one years old when she suddenly developed problems with memory and began to lose the ability to speak and understand what was spoken to her. Her family was very distraught. Dr. Alzheimer treated her until her death in 1906. At her death, the doctor requested permission to perform an autopsy on her. Inside the brain he found many abnormalities. The brain showed shrinkage, especially in the cortex, the outer layer involving memory, thinking, judgment, and speech. He also found widespread fatty deposits in the small blood vessels and abnormal deposits in and around cells. His research was printed in 1907, and in 1910 this brain disorder was named after Dr. Alzheimer.[1]

Fast-forward one hundred years, and we have an unrestrained monster in our midst. In the last century, this disease has gained so much momentum that it is now the seventh leading cause of death in the U.S.[2] At the rate that it is increasing, it could soon be claiming more lives annually than strokes.

Since Alzheimer's is the seventh leading cause of death in the United States, maybe we ought to take a look at who's at risk. According to the *2008 Alzheimer's Disease Facts and Figures* report, 16 percent of women and 11 percent of men over 71 years of age in the U.S. currently have Alzheimer's. The increased percentage of women was attributed to the fact that women generally live longer than men. They have a longer life span in which to develop symptoms. There was no appreciable difference between men and women with the factor of longer life removed.[3]

This same study indicates that people with fewer years of education are at a greater risk than people with more education. A person with less than 12 years of education had a 15 percent greater risk of developing dementia than people with 12–15 years and a 35 percent greater risk than people with over 15 years of education. This could be due to the fact that more education creates a thing called cognitive reserve. Cognitive reserve is the retention of facts, and it either protects from Alzheimer's and other dementias or it allows the person to compensate for a longer period of time before the symptoms of Alzheimer's and dementia are observable.[4]

Exactly, what is this monster of a disease that develops in someone new every 70 seconds?[5] Alzheimer's is the most common form of dementia, accounting for 60–80 percent of all dementia cases.[6] So, let's start with dementia.

Dementia is a progressive decline in cognitive functions. The affected areas may include loss of memory, attention span, language skills, or problem-solving abilities. Some forms of dementia are reversible, depending on the cause. The majority are nonreversible. Some people have dementia from accidents, particularly ones involving head injuries. Other forms are caused by Huntington's disease, hypothyroidism, Parkinson's disease, Vitamin B_1 or B_{12} deficiency, syphilis, hypoglycemia, and many other recognizable diseases. So it's obvious that many forms of dementia have a pathological reason. But of course, there is always the exception. That brings us back to Alzheimer's.

The most common form of dementia has no obvious cause.[7]

Let's look at the symptoms of Alzheimer's disease. The symptoms include memory loss (regarding recently-learned facts), confusion, irritability and aggression, long-term memory loss, and general withdrawal of the patient as their senses decline. Gradually, bodily functions are lost, resulting in death.[8]

Memory Loss

Memory is defined as short-term and long-term. Short-term memory is the ability to correctly recall fairly recent events or learn new material. Long-term memory, LTM, can affect not only memories of childhood and people of the past, but it can also affect recognition of present-day acquaintances. It's as if all history with people close to the patient has been erased. LTM loss affects Alzheimer's patients in the last stages. However, short-term memory loss is one of the first recognizable symptoms of this disease. This is not to be confused with normal, age-related memory loss. As we age, we have a certain amount of memory loss, usually characterized by intermittent incidents, for example, not being able to find the right word to describe what you're thinking or temporarily having a difficult time recalling the name of a casual acquaintance. Alzheimer's-related memory loss involves the inability to remember key pieces of information, like the name of one's spouse or children.

Confusion

Confusion is defined as the loss of orientation. This is the ability to correctly place yourself in the world around you. Confusion creates uncertainty of time, location, and personal identity.

Mood Swings

An Alzheimer's patient will experience severe and rapid mood swings. This includes a level of irritability and aggression never before known to their personality. They can be happy and jolly one minute and ready to bite someone's head off the next. This can sometimes be harder to adjust to than the memory loss, especially if the patient was always a mild-mannered person.

Although Alzheimer's patients display all these symptoms at some point, the severity of the individual's symptoms may vary.

We've looked at the basic symptoms of Alzheimer's from a physical (body) and mental (soul) perspective. Now let's take that final step and look at it from a spiritual perspective.

Chapter 2

WHAT DOES THE BIBLE SAY?

*A Look at the Three Major Symptoms of
Alzheimer's from a Biblical Perspective*

I N THIS CHAPTER, WE WILL BE LOOKING, FIRST OF
all, at the Word of God. Keep this in mind: You can't
base what you believe on your experiences or the experiences of those around you. You can't base what you
believe on your current circumstances or anything that
you see with your natural eyes. You can *only* base what
you believe on the Word of God. We are going to look at
exactly what the Word of God says about the symptoms
of Alzheimer's and prayerfully come to some conclusions
about this disease.

Speaking of prayer, I would like to ask you to stop right
here and pray. Ask the Lord to open the eyes of your understanding. Ask Him to reveal His truth—not my truth or
your truth, but His truth only. Then ask Him to show you
what to do with the truth that He reveals to you.

Now let's see what the Bible says. We will look at the
three main symptom areas from the first chapter. (Words

in brackets are the actual definition of the Hebrew or Greek word.)

Memory

The Bible speaks a great deal about remembering. Most of the references are commands to "forget not." The problem with Alzheimer's is that the patient eventually forgets everything.

> Bless the LORD, O my soul, and forget not all his benefits: Who forgiveth all thine iniquities; who healeth all thy diseases.
>
> —PSALM 103:2–3

We are told to not forget the benefits of the Lord. We are to remember how we were saved and healed. However, even devoted Christians who contract Alzheimer's don't remember how to praise God or speak of His many marvelous works, like salvation and healing.

> …in both which I stir up your pure minds by way of remembrance: That ye be mindful of the words which were spoken before.
>
> —2 PETER 3:1–2

Here is a verse that tells us to be mindful of words spoken before, another memory command. "I stir up your pure minds [deep thoughts] by way of remembrance [to remind quietly, recollection]: That you be mindful [to recall to mind through the idea of *mental grasp*] of the words which were spoken before." This is not just remembering the things we have learned from the Word of God, not just remembering the praises and mighty works of God as commanded in Psalm 103, but also remembering all the words of God throughout the Scriptures. They are words that teach us, correct us, and encourage us; words that answer questions and prayers. These words bring revelation of the deeper things of God.

It seems a shame that all the words of God learned throughout the lifetime of a devoted Christian's life could suddenly be gone and no longer have any usefulness. I know that memory loss is not a choice that someone makes. Nevertheless, it's still heartbreaking to see so much wisdom gained from living a long life suddenly be lost.

Now let's look at a few verses that deal with memory in a different light.

> Get wisdom, get understanding; forget it not; neither decline from the words of my mouth. Forsake her [wisdom] not, and she shall preserve thee; love her, and she shall keep thee.
>
> —PROVERBS 4:5–6

Notice these particular word meanings: "neither decline [bend away] from the words of my mouth. Forsake [relinquish] her not, and she shall preserve [to hedge about as with thorns] thee; love her, and she shall keep [guard, protect, maintain] thee." Now it seems to indicate that when you lose wisdom, you lose the hedge and guard around you. Isn't that what happens in Alzheimer's? When you lose wisdom, understanding, or knowledge—which is all tied up in a person's memory—it seems like all hedges of protection are gone. When that first thread unravels, the complete fabric of a person's being quickly falls apart. In a few short years, they are unrecognizable as the people they truly are.

One more passage of Scripture dealing with memory in an indirect way is Proverbs 3:1–2.

> My son, forget not my law; but let thine heart keep
> my commandments; For length of days, and long
> life, and peace, shall they add to thee.

We are commanded to remember His laws and keep His commandments always. An Alzheimer's patient can't remember the laws of God and most likely will end up breaking quite a few commandments. In the last half of that verse, we see this explained. When you remember His laws and keep His commandments, you will enjoy length of days, long life, and peace.

Now, the first two are all right, but if you have Alzheimer's, length of days and long life aren't that appealing. But, let's look at the word *peace*. In Hebrew, that word literally is *shalom*. It comes from the root word *shalam*, which means "to be safe in mind, body, or estate." That makes length of days and long life worth living!

We see that memory loss is obviously not the Lord's will. He wouldn't tell us so many times to remember and then turn around and cause some people to forget. It's not in the nature of God to be contradictory. So, what does all this mean? Let's examine the other two symptoms of Alzheimer's before we draw any conclusions.

Mood Swings

Personality changes and mood swings may be as hard a symptom to deal with as memory loss. Often an Alzheimer's patient who lived his or her entire life as a sweet-natured, gentle, loving person becomes hateful and belligerent. When you're dealing with Alzheimer's, it's as if you lose the person several times before the end. Mood swings and, particularly, personality changes are to blame for just some of those times.

How do you find information on mood swings and personality changes in the Bible? It's not referred to by those descriptive words. It's usually found in the themes of steadfastness and continuity, which run throughout the Bible.

> Jesus Christ the same yesterday, and to day, and for ever.
>
> —HEBREWS 13:8

> Every good gift and every perfect gift is from above, and cometh down from the Father of lights, with whom is no variableness, neither shadow of turning.
>
> —JAMES 1:17

> For I am the LORD, I change not.
>
> —MALACHI 3:6

I realize that these verses are referring to the Lord, but aren't we supposed to have His characteristics and take on His nature? If we are going to show forth the love of God to this world, we have to be as He is, steadfast and continuous.

> Therefore, my beloved brethren, be ye steadfast, unmoveable, always abounding in the work of the Lord...
>
> —1 CORINTHIANS 15:58

This word *steadfast* means "to be sedentary and settled." We are to always represent the Lord in a consistent manner and lifestyle. The Bible says to be slow to anger and slow to wrath. All these truths point to a person who is consistent, not given to outbursts, a person who is always the same in whatever situation he finds himself.

> For then shalt thou lift up thy face without spot;
> yea, thou shalt be steadfast, and shalt not fear.
>
> —JOB 11:15

In the verse previous to the one above, Job said to put iniquity out of your hand and to not let wickedness dwell in your tabernacle. This word *iniquity* in the Hebrew language means "to exert oneself, usually in vain." It also means "trouble and vanity, specifically regarding idols."

Now, he is saying that if you put aside anything that might not be of God, then you will be steadfast ("to place firmly, stiffen") and will not fear ("be frightened"). We'll talk more about this concept in the next chapter.

> Let not your heart be troubled, neither let it be afraid.
>
> —JOHN 14:27

The word *heart* literally refers to the mind in this verse, and the word translated *troubled* is a Greek word that means "stirred or agitated." So we have a command to keep our minds untroubled and unagitated. When you see a person going through severe mood swings and personality changes, they usually appear troubled and particularly agitated. I think you get the picture here. As children of God, we have a mandate throughout the Scriptures to be consistent in the practice of our faith and our dealings with those around us.

Confusion

There is one more major symptom to digest: confusion. Again, we see this is a symptom of Alzheimer's that is not the Lord's will.

> For God is not the author of confusion, but of peace, as in all the churches of the saints.
> —1 Corinthians 14:33

Looking at the Greek word meanings, we see the following: "God is not the author of confusion [instability, disorder], but of peace [to set at one again, quietness, rest]." Instability and disorder are a good description of an Alzheimer's patient's thought patterns. Remember the definition of *confusion* from chapter 1: "loss of orientation, which is the ability to place oneself correctly in the world by time, location, and personal identity."

> For where envying and strife is, there is confusion and every evil work. But the wisdom that is from above is first pure, then peaceable, gentle, easy to be intreated, full of mercy and good fruits, without partiality, and without hypocrisy. And the fruit of righteousness is sown in peace of them that make peace.
> —James 3:16–18

The words *envying* and *strife* mean "jealousy, envy, and intrigue." The reference to confusion is the same as in

1 Corinthians 14:33; it means "instability and disorder." And the word *peace* is to set at one again.

This is not to say that people with Alzheimer's are full of envying and strife, but the world we live in is overflowing with it. We live in a confusing world. The Bible warns against those that call good evil and evil good, but this very phenomenon is a part of every major headline news item. You have men dressing like women, women trying to be men, children divorcing their parents or killing them, parents throwing away their children—the list goes on and on. Most of these things have run rampant in the last twenty to thirty years.

In the early eighties, as a nineteen-year-old, I watched two soap operas. I would get so frustrated when it was time for my program if my papa was staying at our house while Mama took Granny to the doctor. (It happened more than once.) He would embarrass me by making smooching sounds while the men and women were kissing. I've often wondered how he would react now if he saw men kissing men. I'm convinced it would be worse then smooching sounds.

I'm now in my forties, and I'm astounded at how the world has changed in the last three decades. Confusion and chaos are all about us. How much more astounding is the change in our culture to someone in their late sixties, seventies, or eighties?

I think it's time to draw some conclusions.

Chapter 3

A SOUND MIND

A Look at Our World and the Operation of Fear

Accoding to the *2008 Alzheimer's Facts and Figures* report, the death rate for Alzheimer's rose 44.7 percent between 2000 and 2005.[1] Similarly, in an article that Colm Kelleher, PhD, wrote entitled "Mad Cows, Mad Wildlife, and the Rise of Alzheimer's Disease in North America," the incidence of Alzheimer's in North America has increased 9,000 percent from 1979 to 2004.[2]

Why?

Let's look at the people who turned 65 after 1979. The people born between 1915 and 1935 would have turned sixty-five between 1980 and 2000. What could possibly be different about this group of people to cause the number of Alzheimer's cases to increase exponentially?

We will particularly look at those that were in their fifties and early sixties during the 1980s. This group of people would have been starting to look forward to retirement. They had worked hard their whole lives and enjoyed the fruit of their labors during America's golden age. The 1950s, '60s, and early '70s were prosperous times. The average American didn't get rich, but he lived a far more comfortable life than his parents—and even a lot easier life than he had lived as a child. Life was good, and retirement was going to be great. Then came trouble.

The late 1970s and early 1980s brought inflation, gas shortages, and extremely high interest rates. All of a sudden, the seemingly sufficient amount of Social Security that they were planning to retire on didn't look so sufficient. The cost of living was increasing in leaps and bounds. Could the government keep up with it in Social Security payment increases?

Let's also look at the other important events that would have influenced this group of people. The earlier half of this group was born at the end of World War I. By the time they were fourteen years old, we had the stock market crash of 1929. Worse than the crash itself, with all its horror stories, were the ensuing years of the Great Depression. Now, remember this group either saw the 1929 crash or were born during the depression that followed. Most of them probably grew up extremely hard, just trying to survive.

As America was picking itself back up by the bootstraps, we entered the 1940s and World War II. This seemed like a one-two punch. Many of the young men that saw the country plunge into hard times were now having to ship off to fight a war. However, WWII accomplished a lot, not the least of which was jumpstarting the American economy. The war ended, and this group of people was headed toward better times. Then came the Korean War.

The young men and women who were born during the Great Depression were the ones most affected by the Korean War. It didn't have as large an impact on America as WWII did, but nonetheless, it greatly affected our study group.

After the Korean War, America started suffering through the pains of growth. Civil unrest marked the late 1950s and early '60s. Desegregation was a very volatile but absolutely necessary part of this growth. We could never be the strong nation we were destined to be if we remained divided into two distinct cultures.

With the civil rights movement in full swing, we found ourselves entering the Vietnam War. After WWII, the attitude of the general population of America toward wars and conflicts started changing. By the time we were out of Vietnam, the anti-war sentiment was at its peak. The majority of our study group was not a part of this. They were raised with a strong sense of patriotism. They also had a very definite sense of right and wrong. They had witnessed the evil of Hitler and understood the sacrifice necessary to keep the world safe. The change in the culture and attitudes of the America they grew up in must have been very unsettling.

Also in the '50s and '60s, America experienced the widespread introduction of television. As wonderful as it seemed, TV stations were soon broadcasting more than just *I Love Lucy* and *Red Skelton*. Fearful images of war and unrest in all parts of the globe were flooding into America's living rooms. It was soon obvious that the TV news loved to promote bad stories.

It's even worse now. Have you noticed how they come close to glorifying mass murderers and the like by plastering these stories over the newscast for days at a time? They also make such dire predictions as commentary to their stories that people automatically start fretting over situations and scenarios that aren't even real. The more the media promotes a fear of economic hard times, the more they cause them to actually happen. People become afraid and stop spending their disposable income, they stop borrowing for big purchases, and thus they actually cause the problem that the media instigated through fearful predictions.

Now, back to the late 1970s and early '80s. The rate of change was increasing. It soon hit warp speed with the introduction of the personal computer and hi-tech gadgets. It has been my observation that many people in our study group are distrustful of computers and technology, and some are even fearful of learning to use new technology. So what does all this mean? Let's look at this logically for a few minutes, and then we'll see if our logic lines up with the Word of God—the only logic that matters.

The group of people that experienced a 9,000 percent increase in Alzheimer's during their scheduled retirement years saw incredible world events. It reminds me of the following verse in Luke 21:26:

> Men's hearts failing them for fear, and for looking after those things which are coming on the earth.

The Greek word for "hearts failing" means "to breathe out or faint," but it's from the root word that usually denotes "separation, departure, cessation, etc." It doesn't indicate that this is always a physical departure. It could allude to other types of departure, perhaps even mental.

More specific to this group of people and Alzheimer's in general is 2 Timothy 1:7:

> For God has not given us the spirit of fear; but of power, and of love, and of a sound mind.

Well, there it is in a nutshell. We aren't given a spirit of fear, but a sound mind. Lack of love, lack of power, and lack of a sound mind indicates the presence of a spirit of fear. This doesn't mean the person without love, power, or a sound mind is possessed; but, they are quite possibly being oppressed or tormented.

WHAT IS A SPIRIT OF FEAR?

The Bible says that the enemy of our souls walks about as a roaring lion seeking whom he may devour. (See 1 Peter 5:8.) The enemy is looking for any opening, any chink in the armor that he can invade. Fear is an opening.

There are two different kinds of fear. There is a positive fear that keeps you from walking out into the middle of the highway or sticking your foot in the fireplace to warm it up. This kind of fear is usually an intense respect for something. This is the same kind of fear described in Psalm 111:10: "The fear of the LORD is the beginning of wisdom." It's not that we are frightened or terrified of God, but we do respect His power and who He is. When natural fear gets out of control, a spirit of fear can take over. For example, if you had a loved one who had a minor accident and you became obsessed with not letting that person out of your sight for fear of a worse accident, that's when a natural fear has been taken over by a spirit of fear.

I struggled with a spirit of fear for many years. It started innocently enough. I was walking next door to my cousin's house one evening just as it was getting dark. I was about eight years old, and as I passed the corner of the house, something was underneath my bedroom window. I don't even remember what I saw. Whatever it was took off running through the leaves, and my mama came running in response to my hysterical screams.

After that, as a child I was always afraid to be alone at night and afraid to be out by myself.

As an adult, I would catch my imagination running away with me. I have a very vivid, full-color imagination. I would start running through horrible, tragic scenarios and terrifying *what ifs*. The realization that I was tormented by a spirit of fear came one night as I was sitting in the den. My husband was elsewhere in the house, and suddenly something was moving in the leaves underneath the window behind my chair. (Sound familiar?) I was paralyzed with fear. It turned out just to be a possum, but it did point out my problem. I have since been delivered from the spirit of fear, but we'll discuss that later.

So I know that the spirit of fear is a real thing that walks around with our adversary "seeking whom he may devour." Always remember, fear attracts Satan like blood attracts a shark!

According to Drs. Jerry and Carol Robeson in *Strongman's His Name... What's His Game,* the phrase "fear not" is mentioned in one form or another 365 different times in the Bible.[3] That's one a day for the whole year.

> For ye have not received the spirit of bondage again
> to fear; but ye have received the Spirit of adoption,
> whereby we cry, Abba, Father.
>
> —ROMANS 8:15

The Greek word used for *spirit* both times in this verse means a literal spirit. It has to be either yours, God's, or Satan's. We know that this is a spirit that is received, so we know that it's not your spirit; you already have that. We know that God is not going to put you in bondage, so it must be Satan. *Bondage* literally means "slavery." Being a slave to fear is not from the Lord. You have received the spirit of adoption. In other words, you have received the Holy Spirit of sonship in respect to being adopted by God. We can take from this that God desires for you to live, walk, breathe, and exist inside the spirit realm as adopted sons and daughters of His. He does not desire for you to be entangled again in slavery to fear. Fear is not of God.

Fear is definitely bondage. Fear can paralyze you. It can make you physically sick. It can change you from the person you truly are into a shrinking, shriveling mass of nerves. It will tie you up in a thousand knots. It will ruin your life!

WHY A SPIRIT OF FEAR?

So what evidence do I have that a spirit of fear is behind Alzheimer's? I would never be so bold as to say that 100 percent of Alzheimer's cases are brought on by a spirit of fear. However, I think that the Bible, various survey results, and just good plain common sense indicate that the majority of cases are caused by fear.

A report by Robert J. Buchanan, Suojin Wang, Hyunsu Ju, and David Graber entitled "Analyses of Gender Differences in Profiles of Nursing Home Residents with Alzheimer's Disease" was based on a study of 49,607 nursing home residents who were diagnosed with Alzheimer's. Women accounted for 69.7 percent of the group. The female patients were more likely to be older and widowed.[4] As we discussed earlier in this chapter, these women were the ones that were raised during the Depression and lived most of their lives in America's golden years. The majority of these widowed women would undoubtedly be relying mostly on Social Security for their retirement.

That is a recipe for fear! I witnessed this firsthand. My mama and daddy had been married for forty-seven and one-half years when Daddy died suddenly of an aortic aneurysm. Although Mama was still working and had always been a fairly independent woman, the thought of not having Daddy to take care of certain things was almost overwhelming. Whenever something around the house would tear up or break, I would see her inch toward panic. Even though my husband is a contractor and engineer and can fix most anything, it still took several years for her fearful reflex to subside. Since then she has retired and is relying mostly on Social Security. She is concerned about money, but we refuse to be fearful.

However, many women don't have families that are in

a position to help them. And even if they have the best support network around, they often don't want to burden anyone.

> And seek not ye what ye shall eat, or what ye shall drink, neither be ye of doubtful mind. For all these things do the nations of the world seek after: and your Father knoweth that ye have need of these things. But rather seek ye the kingdom of God; and all these things shall be added unto you. Fear not, little flock; for it is your Father's good pleasure to give you the kingdom.
>
> —LUKE 12:29–32

This is a great set of verses. We are encouraged *not* to worry! One meaning of the term *doubtful mind* is "anxious mind." God is very aware of our physical needs. Now, notice the next command—seek the kingdom of God to have your needs met, but also fear not. It is the Father's will to provide for you. Here is a connection between the idea of money worries and fear.

What about men who are widowed? Well, now that's a little different story. When men are widowed, they do experience a certain amount of fear, but it's not usually a crippling fear. Their fear is often centered more around being lonely. When a woman is widowed, she is concerned with things she doesn't know how to take care of around the house. She might handle being alone fairly well. However, when a man is widowed, he's not concerned about things around the house; he feels the loss in a different way. In a family, it's not so much what a woman does as what she brings to every situation. She is the heart of the home. All the love, care, and concern that she put into every household chore would be evident in its absence. Some men not only lose their wives, but the comfort of their home is unexpectedly gone with her. As sad as this is, it seems that this is not the driving force behind the spirit of fear in men with Alzheimer's.

There are several different ways a spirit of fear could torment men. Let's consider a few of these. First of all, men have a direct command from the Lord to provide for their families and themselves.

> If any provide not for his own and specifically for those of his own house; he hath denied the faith, and is worse than an infidel.
>
> —1 TIMOTHY 5:8

> If any would not work, neither should he eat.
> —2 THESSALONIANS 3:10

This is a very serious responsibility. Unfortunately, in society today this responsibility is not fulfilled as it should be. But our study group took it very seriously. Growing up in America's hard years, these men knew how to work—and work hard. When retirement time came, many of these men found themselves in an unusual position. Suddenly they had no way to provide for themselves or their families. They were reliant on someone else, the government, through Social Security. Although they had earned this money, it was no longer in their control. I can see that with some men it would feel like they weren't fulfilling their responsibilities, making them feel helpless and useless. They had taken care of and provided for their families, they had been the movers and shakers of society, and then they retired. This can make a man feel that he is no longer needed. All these feelings can lead to fear. One of the most common fears of mankind is the fear of not being needed.

Retired men have more time to think than they've ever had. Without the time confines of an everyday job, the hours can drag by. More time to think can be good. If their thoughts turn toward God and family, they will enjoy the well-earned benefits of retirement. If their thoughts turn inward and accusing, continually concerned with how to live without a paycheck, then they will open the door to the spirit of fear.

I think that there are other things that come into play with the spirit of fear. So many things seem to slip by us when it comes to obeying the Word of God and following His examples and guidelines. Now, I try to not get carried away with any one thing, but I try to take the whole Word of God and look at all aspects of a problem.

However, there is one Bible principle in particular that we, as Christians, seem to overlook.

We are made in the image of God. According to the Book of Genesis, God spoke and the world came into existence. Because we are made in His image, our words also have creative power. We create situations and atmospheres with our words. The argument might be offered that people really don't mean what they say, that usually they are just joking around. That's where we miss it. Our words are very important and should be thought through before they are spoken. I love to joke around, but I'm very conscious of not casually speaking destructive things in fun.

Jesus said in Mark 11:23, "Whosoever shall say unto this mountain, Be thou removed, and be thou cast into the sea; and shall not doubt in his heart, but shall believe that those things which he saith shall come to pass; he shall have whatsoever he saith." This is a spiritual principle. It informs us how much power our words have. I can see how a Christian who is ignorant of how important their words are could say things and think that they are just silly words. But they are not just words.

> But I say unto you, That every idle [inactive, unemployed, useless] word that men shall speak, they shall give account [reasoning, motive] thereof in the day of judgment.
>
> —MATTHEW 12:36

An idle word is a word that is not working, or simply put, it is a faithless word. For example, when people forget things, they may say, "I must have Alzheimer's." Believe me, you don't want it, so why say something so silly? Continually speaking things like this will introduce a spirit of fear into your life. If you say it long enough, you will start wondering if maybe you really do have Alzheimer's. Then there are the people whose parents died of cancer, and they are constantly saying, "My parents died of cancer. That's the way I'll probably go too." Is that the way you want to go? Not me. I want to go with the Lord when He comes back. And if that's not in my lifetime, I'd rather die of laughter on my ninetieth birthday! Don't say things you don't mean. Don't entertain thoughts of destruction.

They aren't just words. They are openings in the armor. They are invitations for attack.

Remember what Job said in Job 3:25: "For the thing which I greatly feared is come upon me, and that which I was afraid of is come unto me." It is possible that Job gave the enemy too much information. If he had been speaking his fears, then Satan knew where to attack to hurt him the most. Don't give the enemy anything to work with. If you give him an inch, he will become your ruler. Be responsible for what you say, and even before you say it take those thoughts captive! (See 2 Corinthians 10:5.) Become a man or woman of faith. Let the words of your mouth speak of a faith-filled trust in the Lord. (See Psalm 19:14.) Build up with your words and refuse to tear down.

The Book of James gives us a little more insight into how dangerous the tongue can be.

> So also the tongue is a small part of the body, and yet it boasts of great things See how great a forest is set aflame by such a small fire! And the tongue is a fire, the very world of iniquity; the tongue is set among our members as that which defiles the entire body, and sets on fire the course of our life, and is set on fire by hell. For every species of beasts and birds, of reptiles and creatures of the sea, is tamed and has been tamed by the human race. But no one can tame the tongue; it is a restless evil and full of deadly poison. With it we bless our Lord and Father, and with it we curse men, who have been made in the likeness of God; from the same mouth come both blessing and cursing. My brethren, these things ought not to be this way.
>
> —JAMES 3:5–10, NAS

For a Christian, speaking out faithless words and praising the Lord at the same time is not profitable. It sends a mixed message to the world about our wonderful Lord. These things "ought not to be."

There are many verses in the Bible regarding the

tongue. It's enough to make you want to be very careful about what you say.

> Death and life are in the power of the tongue, And those who love it will eat its fruit.
>
> —PROVERBS 18:21, NAS

> He who guards his mouth and his tongue, Guards his soul from troubles.
>
> —PROVERBS 21:23, NAS

> The one who guards his mouth preserves his life; The one who opens wide his lips comes to ruin.
>
> —PROVERBS 13:3, NAS

> For 'The one who desires life, to love and see good days, must keep his tongue from evil and his lips from speaking deceit.'
>
> —1 PETER 3:10, NAS

All these verses scream for us to keep a guard on our words. Words have power. We are told that death and life, staying out of trouble, preserving one's life, enjoying life and love, and seeing good days are all tied up in how you take authority over your mouth.

Don't speak out fearful imaginations. Remember your enemy, as a roaring lion, walks around looking for someone he can devour. Our words attract him, and our self-centered, not Christ-centered, attitudes allow him to devour. Do not be fearful.

Fear is a thief. It will rob you of many things. Have you ever heard of a witness in a murder trial who was threatened? A witness can be scared into not testifying to the truth. In the same way, we are witnesses in a large-scale courtroom. We are called to testify of Jesus' sacrifice and God's mighty works. If fear, through Alzheimer's, can keep us from testifying, then the enemy will have accomplished half his purpose.

The other purpose of the enemy is found in Deuteronomy 4:9:

> Only give heed to yourself and keep your soul diligently, so that you do not forget the things which your eyes have seen and they do not depart from your heart all the days of your life; but make them known to your sons and your grandsons. (NAS)

Passing on the knowledge of the Lord to one's children and grandchildren is impossible with Alzheimer's. With Alzheimer's you "forget the things which your eyes have seen and they…depart from your heart." When this happens, the enemy's mission is accomplished.

It's no coincidence that the incidence of Alzheimer's has risen so steeply in the last thirty years. Because we are so close to the End Times, there has never been a more urgent need for the wisdom and guidance of the mature saints of God. They have so much to offer the church in this last battle, but their families and churches are being robbed of their leadership and wisdom.

> The thief comes only to steal and kill and destroy; I came that they may have life, and have it abundantly.
>
> —JOHN 10:10, NAS

How long will we tolerate the attacks of an enemy that we already have victory over through the blood of Jesus?

> My people are destroyed for lack of knowledge.
>
> —HOSEA 4:6, NAS

Chapter 4

GUARDING AGAINST
A SPIRIT OF FEAR

A Look at Hope

THE BIBLE SAYS IN PROVERBS 22 THAT THE prudent man sees evil coming and hides himself. So if you recognize this as the truth, you will hide yourself from fear. But where do you hide? The only place we have to hide. The only place where the enemy can't touch us—under His wings. Look at some of the many times we are encouraged to hide.

> Keep me as the apple of the eye; Hide me in the shadow of your wings.
>
> —PSALM 17:8, NAS

> For in the day of trouble He will conceal me in His tabernacle; In the secret place of His tent He will hide me.
>
> —PSALM 27:5, NAS

You hide them in the secret place of Your presence from the conspiracies of man; You keep them secretly in a shelter from the strife of tongues.

—PSALM 31:20, NAS

You are my hiding place; You preserve me from trouble; You surround me with songs of deliverance.

—PSALM 32:7, NAS

Hear my voice, O God, in my prayer: preserve my life from fear of the enemy. Hide me from the secret counsel of the wicked; from the insurrection of the workers of iniquity.

—PSALM 64:1–2

You are my hiding place and my shield; I wait for Your word.

—PSALM 119:114, NAS

Deliver me, O LORD, from mine enemies: I flee unto thee to hide me.

—PSALM 143:9

When you were a young child, if you were walking through a dark forest you would cling to your dad. As you got into those adolescent years, you would start acting brave and self-sufficient. (This is usually where we get into trouble). But the farther you go and the more you mature, you start seeing the dangers of this dark world that we live in, and you understand the wisdom of sticking really close to "Dad."

But how do I stick close to or hide in God? This question brings us back to trust. Fear enters in when we neglect to fully trust in God. We live in a self-sufficient society. We tend to rely on our own strength more than God's and trust in our own abilities more than God's.

> In thee, O Lord, do I put my trust: let me never be put to confusion.
>
> —Psalm 71:1

> Thou wilt keep him in perfect peace, whose mind is stayed on thee: because he trusteth in thee. Trust ye in the Lord forever: for in the Lord Jehovah is everlasting strength [figuratively, a refuge].
>
> —Isaiah 26:3–4

In this second verse Isaiah connects three ideas for us. God will keep in peace ("welfare of health, prosperity, peace") the one whose mind is stayed ("to take hold of") on Him because this person trusts ("to run for refuge; be confident, sure") in the Lord. In these verses, the welfare of our health and prosperity is directly connected to keeping our minds on the Lord and trusting Him.

> He who dwells in the shelter of the Most High Will abide in the shadow of the Almighty. I will say to the Lord, "My refuge and my fortress, My God, in

35

whom I trust!" For it is He who delivers you from the snare of the trapper And from the deadly pestilence. He will cover you with His pinions, And under His wings you may seek refuge; His faithfulness is a shield and bulwark. You will not be afraid of the terror by night, Or of the arrow that flies by day; Of the pestilence that stalks in darkness, Or of the destruction that lays waste at noon. A thousand may fall at your side And ten thousand at your right hand, But it shall not approach you. You will only look on with your eyes And see the recompense of the wicked. For you have made the LORD, my refuge, Even the Most High, your dwelling place. No evil will befall you, Nor will any plague come near your tent.

—PSALM 91:1–10, NAS

Trust in the LORD with all thine heart; and lean not unto thine own understanding. In all thy ways acknowledge him, and he shall direct thy paths. Be not wise in thine own eyes: fear the LORD, and depart from evil. It shall be health to thy navel, and marrow to thy bones.

—PROVERBS 3:5–8

The fear of man bringeth a snare: but whoso putteth his trust in the LORD shall be safe.

—PROVERBS 29:25

Look at Psalm 91:1–10. These promises are incredible. Your part is to dwell in the shelter of the Most High and abide in the shadow of the Almighty. If you do that, just look at what is promised to you. What a deal! You are promised refuge and protection from the Lord, and deliverance from those trying to trap you, deadly pestilence (disease), and evil. Two more times you are promised protection from disease. But you must first do your part—dwell in the shelter of the Most High.

The Bible is full of verses directing us to always cling to the Lord or dwell in His shelter. Because we are so very close to the return of the Lord, the "woods" get darker with every passing day. Cling to "Dad."

> Behold, God is my salvation; I will trust, and not be afraid: for the LORD JEHOVAH is my strength and my song; he also is become my salvation.
> —ISAIAH 12:2

This is especially for the widows:

> Now she that is a widow indeed, and desolate, trusteth in God, and continueth in supplications and prayers night and day.
> —1 TIMOTHY 5:5

We need to cling to the Lord continually, but particularly as we slow down in retirement. I know many retired people who haven't slowed down, but they have the opportunity to take more time with the Lord. Drawing closer to the Lord has many benefits, not only for health, but safety, wisdom, and discernment. These benefits are helpful throughout life. The wisdom and discernment from this time with Him would particularly come in handy during the working, family-rearing years. It seems that during that time of life, we often fall into the category of the seed that fell among thorns (the cares of this world), which sprang up and choked the Word and made it unfruitful. (See Matthew 13:3–23.) It is imperative that we live a life of dependence upon the Lord at all times and seasons of our lives.

It is clear in the Scriptures that clinging to the Lord is for our benefit.

> Beloved, I pray that in all respects you may prosper and be in good health, just as your soul prospers.
> —3 JOHN 2, NAS

> Grace and peace be multiplied unto you through the knowledge of God, and of Jesus our Lord, According as his divine power hath given unto us all things that pertain unto life and godliness, through the knowledge of him that hath called us to glory and virtue: Whereby are given unto us exceeding great and precious promises: that by these ye might be partakers of the divine nature, having escaped the corruption that is in the world through lust.
> —2 PETER 1:2–4

> Study to shew thyself approved [acceptable] unto
> God, a workman that needeth not to be ashamed,
> rightly dividing the word of truth.
>
> —2 TIMOTHY 2:15

For additional reading, look at Deuteronomy 28. As you read this, keep in mind, these are promises to those who obey His words and commandments and don't worship idols. You may be thinking that nobody worships idols in our society. "Why, we're a God-fearing nation!" you might say. Are you sure? An idol isn't necessarily a heathen god of wood or stone. An idol is anything you put in front of God. We have many idols in this country. Probably the most worshiped is "self," followed closely by "money," "success," and "fame." Matthew 6:24 proves this point.

> No one can serve two masters; for either he will
> hate the one and love the other, or he will be
> devoted to one and despise the other. You cannot
> serve God and wealth. (NAS)

The conclusion is, the only way you're going to get through this life in one piece is to cling, cling, cling to the Lord. We need to stick so close to the Lord that if He stops we bump into Him.

This is the way I illustrate it in my teachings on healing: imagine yourself strolling arm in arm, side by side, with the Lord through the universe. He's holding a large umbrella that covers both of you. That's odd, but it doesn't matter because you're with the Lord. You're having a nice walk, when suddenly you see something off to the right that you'd like to look at. You would have to leave His side to see it up close, but it wouldn't be for long. And besides, it was just a few feet away from Him. If looks so inviting that you just *have* to see it, so you take the chance. You let go of God and run out from under His umbrella.

It doesn't take long to figure out what the umbrella was for. There's stuff falling down all over out there! You're soon getting pummeled right and left. Worry, fear, lust, control, and countless other nasty things are beating you down. If only you hadn't left the safety of God and His umbrella. Can you run back? Will He let you under His protective umbrella when you were dumb enough to leave it in the first place?

Yes, this story can have a happy ending. You *can* get back. Run back to the safety of the Lord. You are bruised and battered, and you will most likely bear some scars for your poor choices. But, you don't have to continue to get hurt. He is waiting for you and longing for your return. Just like you would welcome back one of your children who had walked, or even run, away from you!

Thank God we serve the God of second chances. *Cling to Him.*

There is no fear in love; but perfect love casteth out fear; because fear hath torment, He that feareth is not made perfect in love. We love him, because he first loved us.

—1 John 4:18–19

God loves you more than you could possibly love Him. *Trust Him. Cling to Him.*

Chapter 5

IF ALZHEIMER'S IS ALREADY PRESENT

A Look at the Healer

I F YOU HAVE BEEN DIAGNOSED WITH ALZHEIMER'S and your thinking is still clear enough, start praying and studying today. Keep your mind occupied with the Word of the Lord. Turn off the television, and read, read, read! Study and pray as if your very life depended on it—because it does.

Start each day with the armor of God prayer at the end of this book. This is a spiritual battle that you are in, so you need all the armor you can get! You need to also pray, rebuking the spirit of fear. Below is a good sample prayer taken from *Strongman's His Name... What's His Game?*

> *Father, I see that fear is not from You. I under-*
> *stand that fear, worry, and doubt are the*
> *negative faith of the enemy. Forgive me for ever*
> *doubting Your ability to watch over and care*

for me. I will trust You from this time forth as my Source of security.

Satan, in the name of Jesus, I bind your spirit of fear according to Matthew 18:18 that says very clearly, "…whatsoever ye shall bind on earth shall be bound in heaven." I will not stand for your attacks of fear. Leave me alone, this very instant, and never return. If you try, I'll use the Sword of the Spirit against you.

Thank you, Lord Jesus, for Your Peace, Power, Love and Sound Mind. I loose Your Holy Spirit in my life according to Matthew 18:18 that promises, "…whatsoever ye shall loose on earth shall be loosed in heaven." I refuse to allow fear to rob me of all the good things You have for Your children. I claim the mind of Christ from this day forward. Thank you for delivering me from fear. Amen.[1]

If you are reading this book because you have a loved one that has Alzheimer's, start with the prayer above, rebuking the spirit of fear. Engage the Alzheimer's patient in this process as much as their disability will allow. As a child of God, it would be more effective for them to pray for themselves and take authority in Christ. However, if they are too advanced, you may have to go to battle for them by yourself.

Although the Bible doesn't have specific guidelines

about standing in faith on behalf of someone else, we do have several general principles that we can follow. We are commanded to lift up one another and pray for each other. More specifically, several times Jesus healed people when someone else asked for them. For example, Jarius asked for his daughter's healing and the Roman centurion asked for his servant's. In these cases, both of those in need were dependents of the one requesting the healing. If your loved one is advanced to the point that you are standing in prayer for them, then it seems that they are dependent upon you.

Always remember, you are praying to Jehovah-rapha, the God that heals. This is a covenant name, which means it is a promise of God for those with whom He is in covenant. It is the very nature and character of God to heal.

> Bless the LORD, O my soul....who healeth all thy diseases.
>
> —PSALM 103:2–3

> If thou wilt diligently hearken to the voice of the LORD thy God, and wilt do that which is right in his sight, and wilt give ear to his commandments, and keep all his statutes, I will put none of these diseases upon thee, which I have brought upon the Egyptians: for I am the LORD that healeth thee.
>
> —EXODUS 15:26

> Who his own self bare our sins in his own body
> on the tree, that we, being dead to sins, should
> live unto righteousness: by whose stripes ye were
> healed.
>
> —1 Peter 2:24

Notice the use of the past tense in the previous verse, as if you've already been healed. Your healing was paid for on Calvary, so you have already been healed.

> Surely he hath borne our griefs, and carried our
> sorrows: yet we did esteem him stricken, smitten
> of God, and afflicted. But he was wounded for our
> transgressions, he was bruised for our iniquities:
> the chastisement of our peace was upon him; and
> with his stripes we are healed.
>
> —Isaiah 53:4–5

Notice the use of the present tense there, which was used before Christ was even born.

According to Scripture, it is God's perfect will to heal His children. I have not found one single example in the Scriptures in which God did not heal when asked. Many people think that Paul was that one example. However, there is enough controversy around Paul's "thorn" that it's not a valid reason for disbelief in God's will to heal. (I personally think that Paul's thorn was not physical but was, in fact, his great love for his fellow Jews. That's what won him the many beatings that he got.)

45

As I said, I believe the Scriptures bear out the fact that it is God's perfect will to heal. But, we don't live in a perfect world. We subject ourselves to many things in life that are not God's will for us. Some of these I have touched on in this book. If healing is eluding you, there are a few more things that you need to ask yourself.

Perhaps the biggest hindrance to healing is unforgiveness. There is the story in the Book of Matthew that tells of the man who was deeply indebted to the king. He appeared before the king and begged for mercy. The king had mercy on him and forgave his enormous debt. This man who had just been forgiven so much went directly out into the street and ran into a man who owed him a measly amount of money. The man couldn't pay and begged for mercy, but the recently-forgiven man gave him none. He had the man thrown into debtor's prison. When the king heard what the recently-forgiven man had done, he had the man brought before him. The king was so angry that he had the man thrown into prison and "turned him over to the tormentors."

As followers of Christ, we have been forgiven an enormous debt, a debt that was impossible to pay, a debt that had us bound—and bound for hell, at that. Who are you not to forgive that person who owes you a measly sum compared with the debt that you've been forgiven? Do not live in unforgiveness. You can't afford to. When you hold unforgiveness in your heart toward someone, it is not hurting them, it is only hurting you! Unforgiveness will drive a wedge between you and the promises of God, which you so desperately need. Live a life of forgiveness, and let God deal with the person who has wronged you. He is much more effective. It's kind of like a parent settling an argument between two pouting children. One child may have a very good reason to be upset at the other. Likewise, you may have a legitimate reason for being upset at someone, but no adult has a good reason to act like a child.

If healing still eludes you after checking your forgiveness level, then you also need to get alone with the Lord and make absolute certain that there is nothing standing between you and Him, anything like unconfessed sin or lack of belief. To see your healing manifested in your body, you need to get very serious with and very close to God. This isn't a magic lamp that you rub to get what you want. This is a lifestyle, mind-set, heart state, and paradigm shift.

Start living life to the fullest right now by clinging to the Lord!

CONCLUSION

I PRAY THIS BOOK HAS PROVIDED YOU WITH SOME helpful information. Let it also be an encouragement to you to draw closer to the Lord. If you're reading this book and you don't really know this person called Jesus, we can fix that right now. You see, God's promises are particularly for His children. He has blessed and healed people who are not His children on many occasions; however, His promises are for His children. It's kind of like you and your family. You are obligated to feed your children, but I'm sure there have been many times that you've fed your children's friends. You wouldn't deny them food, but it's not your duty to feed them. It's the same with God. As wonderful as God's promises are, the best reason to come into a personal relationship with Him is so that you can know Him eternally.

This life is like the steam coming off a teakettle; it only lasts a little while. Eternity, now that's a different story. Where you live throughout eternity depends on what you do with Jesus Christ in this life. The death, burial, and resurrection of Jesus Christ is an event that everyone must respond to in one way or the other. Because God is holy, He can't bear to have sin in His presence. For you to live in His presence throughout eternity, you have to have your sins hidden from sight. The only way to do this is to hide them under the blood of Jesus Christ.

Our sins carry the penalty of death. Someone has to pay with his or her life. Jesus gladly came and paid the death penalty for our sins so that we wouldn't have to, so you have a choice. You can either accept the fact that Jesus died in your place, or you can pay your own penalty and die yourself for all eternity. Personally, I would rather live than die. What about you?

Coming into a right relationship with God through His Son, Jesus, is not a really complicated thing. It is basically you admitting that you need help and taking the help that He so generously offers. Below is a sample prayer. You can use this prayer or you can pray in your own words. This is a guideline of the basic things you need to cover with God. Prayer is just talking to God like you would talk to a respected elder. Remember, these are not magic words. They won't do you any good unless you sincerely mean what you are praying.

> *Dear heavenly Father, I come to You admitting that I am a sinner in need of a Savior. Father, thank You for giving Your only Son to die in my place so that I could be reconciled to You. Please forgive me of my sins. Jesus, I ask You to come into my life and be my Savior and Lord.*

Father, I thank You that by the blood of Jesus I am now one of Your children. Amen.

Now that you are a child of God, start reading the letter He wrote to you, the Bible. In it you will find all sorts of promises to His children—*to you!*

Always remember, we are in a battle. Your enemy is "walking about as a roaring lion seeking whom he may devour." You determine if he devours you or not. Jump headfirst into the Word of God.

DON'T LET UP.

DON'T GIVE UP.

WE DON'T HAVE MUCH TIME LEFT.

HE'S COMING SOON!

Armor of God Prayer

Good morning, Father! Good morning, Jesus! Good morning, Holy Spirit!

Today, heavenly Father, according to Your Word, I present my body a living sacrifice, holy and acceptable in Your sight. Because I am not contending against flesh and blood but against principalities, powers, world rulers of this present darkness, and spiritual hosts of wickedness in heavenly places, I take on the whole armor of God so that I may be able to withstand in the evil day. So today I stand and gird my loins with truth. I put on the breastplate of righteousness. I shod my feet with the preparation of the gospel of peace. Above all these, I take the shield of faith to quench all the flaming darts of the evil one. I take the helmet of salvation and the sword of the Spirit, which is the Word of God.

I pray at all times in the Spirit with all prayer and supplication for all God's family and for me, that I may open my mouth boldly to proclaim the gospel. The weapons of my warfare are not worldly but have divine power to destroy strongholds. Today I destroy arguments and every proud obstacle to the knowledge of God and take every thought captive to obey Christ.

Thank You, Father, that according to Your Word the glory of the Lord is my rear guard. I praise You and thank You for the armor of light You've provided for me this day. I am completely covered now. Upon Jesus I have built my life. The gates of hell shall not prevail against me.

Jesus, I apply Your precious blood to my life, my family, my home, and all my possessions. You are my Shepherd, and I shall not want, for You have supplied all my needs according to Your riches in glory. I can do all things through Christ who strengthens me. I praise You for walking in divine health, for You are my God who heals all my diseases. I praise You and thank You for my prosperity and good health, even as my soul prospers, for the joy of the Lord is my strength.

Father, I have prayed according to Your Word. You said You would watch over Your Word to perform it. I am reminded that every word spoken becomes a living thing—either to minister life or death and destruction.

Lord Jesus, let my meditation be sweet to You, as I will rejoice in You all day. Just rise up and live big within me, for I am Yours and You are mine. In the mighty name of Jesus, amen.

NOTES

CHAPTER 1
WHAT IS ALZHEIMER'S?

1. "About Dr. Alzheimer," Alzheimer's Association, *Alzheimer's Association*, http://www.alz.org/alzheimers_disease_what_is_alzheimers.asp#Alzheimer (accessed July 22, 2009).

2. Ibid.

3. Alzheimer's Association, *2008 Alzheimer's Disease Facts and Figures, National Adult Day Services Association*, http://www.nadsa.org/publications/documents/2008_Alzheimers_Facts_web.pdf (accessed July 22, 2009).

4. Ibid.

5. "Alzheimer's Facts and Figures," Alzheimer's Association, *Alzheimer's Association*, http://www.alz.org/alzheimers_disease_facts_figures.asp (accessed July 22, 2009).

6. "Related Dementias," Alzheimer's Association, *Alzheimer's Association*, http://www.alz.org/alzheimers_disease_related_diseases.asp (accessed July 22, 2009).

7. Ibid.

8. "Alzheimer's disease," *www.Wikipedia.com*, http://en.wikipedia.org/wiki/Alzheimer's_disease (accessed July 23, 2009).

CHAPTER 3
A SOUND MIND

1. *2008 Alzheimer's Disease Facts and Figures.*

2. Colm Kelleher, "Mad Cows, Mad Wildlife, and the Rise of Alzheimer's Disease in North America," *VegSource.com*, June 12, 2005, http://www.vegsource.com/articles2/kelleher_13things_print.htm (accessed July 23, 2009).

3. Drs. Jerry and Carol Robeson, *Strongman's His Name . . . What's His Game?* New Kensington, PA: Whitaker House, 2000.

4. Robert J. Buchanan, Suojin Wang, Hyunsu Ju, and David Graber, "Analyses of Gender Differences in Profiles of Nursing Home Residents with Alzheimer's Disease," *Gender Medicine* vol. 1, issue 1 (August 2004): pp. 48–59, http://www.sciencedirect.com/science?_ob=ArticleURL&_udi=B7MDM-4DPSMP6-8&_user=10&_rdoc=1&_fmt=&_orig=search&_sort=d&_docanchor=&view=c&_acct=C000050221&_version=1&_urlVersion=0&_userid=10&md5=5231091f553630b9507b14a03fe32970 (accessed July 23, 2009).

CHAPTER 5
IF ALZHEIMER'S IS ALREADY PRESENT

1. Robeson.

To Contact the Author

alzthereishope@gmail.com